THE ART OF PAPER QUILLING

Mastering Techniques & Designs

RODNEY SMITH

Copyright © 2024

Table Of Contents

Introduction To Paper Quilling

What is Paper Quilling?

Paper quilling, also known as paper filigree, is a captivating art form that involves rolling, coiling, and shaping thin strips of paper into intricate designs. This craft transforms simple paper into stunning works of art, ranging from delicate floral patterns to elaborate three-dimensional sculptures. Known for its elegance and versatility, quilling allows artists to create everything from handmade greeting cards and jewelry to home décor and framed wall art.

One of the most appealing aspects of paper quilling is its accessibility. With just a few basic tools—a quilling tool, paper strips, and glue—beginners can quickly learn foundational techniques and start creating beautiful designs. As they gain confidence, they can explore more complex methods like husking, fringing, and layering to add texture and depth to their creations. The art form encourages patience, precision, and creativity, making it both a relaxing hobby and a rewarding way to express oneself.

Rooted in centuries-old traditions, quilling has a fascinating history that adds depth to its practice. Originating in Renaissance Europe and spreading across the world, it was once used to imitate metal filigree in religious art. Today, quilling has evolved into a global craft, practiced by artists and hobbyists alike who continue to innovate and push the boundaries of this timeless art.

Whether you're drawn to quilling for its artistic potential, meditative qualities, or the joy of handmade creation, this craft offers a unique way to transform simple materials into meaningful, beautiful works of art. With each twist and turn of the paper, quilling invites you into a world of creativity where possibilities are endless and every piece tells a story.

CHAPTER 1

History And Introduction

Paper quilling, also known as paper filigree, has a rich and fascinating history that dates back several centuries. The origins of quilling are often traced to the Renaissance period in Europe, where nuns and monks are believed to have created decorative designs using thin strips of paper. These strips were often curled, coiled, and shaped to mimic the intricate metal filigree that adorned religious objects. Quilling provided an affordable alternative to gold or silver filigree, allowing artists to create elegant decorations using humble materials.

In the 18th century, paper quilling gained popularity across Europe, particularly among aristocratic women who used it to embellish book covers, picture frames, furniture, and even to create delicate wall art. Quilling became known as a "ladies' pastime," with the art being practiced by genteel women as a refined and respectable hobby. It spread to the American colonies, where quilling continued to be a popular decorative art form, often taught in boarding schools to young women.

The art of quilling has evolved significantly over the centuries, moving from religious contexts to become a global craft enjoyed by artists and hobbyists alike. In recent years, there has been a resurgence of interest in quilling, with contemporary artists pushing the boundaries of the art form to create stunning and complex designs. Modern quilling incorporates a variety of techniques and styles, blending traditional methods with innovative approaches to produce vibrant, dimensional artworks.

Today, quilling is celebrated as a versatile and accessible art form that combines creativity with precision. It remains a popular craft worldwide, cherished for its history, adaptability, and the unique, handcrafted beauty of each piece.

Application

1. **Home Decor**: Create unique wall art, framed pieces, and decorative accents for your home.

2. **Greeting Cards and Stationery**: Design custom cards, invitations, and envelopes with intricate quilled motifs.

3. **Jewelry Making**: Craft one-of-a-kind earrings, pendants, and bracelets using quilled elements.

4. **Gift Wrapping**: Embellish gift boxes, bags, and tags with delicate quilled designs for a personalized touch.

5. **Scrapbooking**: Add dimension and interest to scrapbook layouts with quilled embellishments and borders.

6. **Ornaments and Decorations**: Make ornaments for holidays and special occasions, or create hanging mobiles and window decorations.

7. **Mixed Media Art**: Combine quilling with other art mediums such as painting, collage, and embroidery for unique mixed media pieces.

8. **Educational Projects**: Use quilling as a hands-on learning tool in classrooms to teach geometry, patterns, and creativity.

9. **Fashion and Accessories**: Incorporate quilled elements into clothing, accessories, and hair ornaments for a distinctive look.

10. **Art Therapy**: Utilize paper quilling as a therapeutic activity to reduce stress, improve focus, and enhance mental well-being.

These are just a few examples of how paper quilling can be applied creatively in various aspects of life, allowing artists to express themselves and add beauty to the world around them.

Materials and Tools

1. **Quilling Paper Strips**: These come in various widths, lengths, and colors. Choose acid-free paper for longevity.

2. **Adhesive**: Use a fine-tip glue applicator or clear-drying craft glue to secure your quilled shapes.

3. **Quilling Board**: A corkboard with grid lines helps in creating uniform shapes and sizes.

4. **Quilling Tool**: The most common tool is a slotted quilling tool, but you can also use a needle tool or tweezers for different techniques.

5. **Ruler and Cutting Mat**: For measuring and cutting your paper strips accurately.

6. **Scissors**: Sharp, small scissors for cutting paper strips to size.

7. **Tweezers**: Useful for handling small quilled pieces and intricate designs.

8. **Paper Cutter**: Optional but handy for cutting straight and even strips of paper.

9. **Embellishments**: Beads, sequins, rhinestones, and other decorative elements to enhance your quilled creations.

10. **Protective Sealant**: A clear spray or brush-on sealant to protect your finished pieces from dust and moisture.

Optional Materials:

1. **Quilling Comb**: Creates unique combing effects and patterns in your quilling designs.

2. **Circle Sizer Ruler**: Helps in making consistently sized coils and circles.

3. **Quilling Mold**: Used for shaping and forming 3D quilled shapes.

4. **Parchment Paper**: Prevents your quilled shapes from sticking to surfaces while drying.

5. Pattern Books or Templates: Provide inspiration and guidance for creating specific designs and motifs.

6. **Storage Containers:** Keep your quilling supplies organized and easily accessible.

With these materials and tools, you'll be well-equipped to dive into the world of paper quilling and unleash your creativity.

CHAPTER 2

Basic Techniques

Rolling

Materials:

- Quilling paper strips
- Quilling tool (slotted or needle)
- Adhesive

Steps:

1. Select a quilling paper strip of your desired color and width.

2. Insert one end of the strip into the slot of the quilling tool.

3. Hold the other end of the strip between your thumb and index finger.

4. Roll the quilling tool towards you, guiding the paper strip with your fingers.

5. Continue rolling until you reach the end of the strip.

6. Carefully remove the rolled coil from the quilling tool.

7. Apply a small amount of adhesive to the end of the strip to secure the coil in place.

Coiling

Materials:

- Quilling paper strips
- Quilling tool (slotted or needle)
- Adhesive

Steps:

1. Start with a quilling paper strip.

2. Place the end of the strip onto the quilling tool, leaving a tail for gluing later.
3. Rotate the quilling tool to coil the paper strip around itself.

4. Keep coiling until you reach your desired size or shape.

5. Carefully slide the coil off the quilling tool.

6. Apply adhesive to the end of the strip and press it firmly to secure the coil.

Shaping

Materials:

- Quilling paper strips
- Quilling tool (slotted or needle)

- Adhesive

Steps:

1. Begin with a coiled quilling shape.

2. Use your fingers or a quilling mold to gently shape and manipulate the coil into desired forms.

3. Press and hold the coil in place until it retains its shape.

4. Experiment with different shaping techniques to create various designs and patterns.

5. Secure any loose ends with adhesive if necessary.

Creating Loose Coils

Materials:

- Quilling paper strips
- Quilling tool (slotted or needle)
- Adhesive

Steps:

1. Start with a quilling paper strip.

2. Hold one end of the strip and insert the other end into the quilling tool.

3. Rotate the quilling tool to coil the paper strip loosely around itself.

4. Keep coiling until you reach your desired size.

5. Carefully slide the coil off the quilling tool.
6. Pinch one end of the coil to form a teardrop or oval shape.

7. Apply adhesive to the pinched end to secure the loose coil in place.

Tight Coils

Materials:

- Quilling paper strips
- Quilling tool (slotted or needle)
- Adhesive

Steps:
1. Start with a quilling paper strip.

2. Hold one end of the strip and insert the other end into the quilling tool.

3. Rotate the quilling tool to coil the paper strip tightly around itself.

4. Keep coiling until you reach your desired size.

5. Carefully slide the coil off the quilling tool.
6. Apply adhesive to the end of the strip to secure the tight coil in place.

These basic techniques form the foundation of paper quilling and can be combined and expanded upon to create more complex designs and patterns. Experiment with different colors, shapes, and sizes to unleash your creativity!

CHAPTER 3

Intermediate Project

Marquise or Eye Shape:

Materials:

- Quilling paper strips
- Quilling tool (slotted or needle)
- Adhesive

Steps:

1. Start with a loose coil or tight coil as a base.

2. Pinch one end of the coil to create a point.
3. Pinch the opposite end of the coil to create a teardrop or oval shape.

4. Adjust the shape and size as desired, making sure both ends are symmetrical.

5. Apply adhesive to the pinched points to secure the marquise or eye shape.

Fringed Flowers:

Materials:

- Quilling paper strips
- Quilling tool (slotted or needle)
- Adhesive

Steps:

1. Start with a tight coil as the center of the flower.

2. Cut multiple quilling paper strips into small pieces, about 1 inch long.

3. Apply adhesive around the outer edge of the tight coil.

4. Press the cut paper pieces onto the adhesive, spacing them evenly around the coil.

5. Gently curl the fringed strips outward to create a flower-like effect.

6. Continue adding and curling strips until the desired fullness is achieved.

S-scrolls:

Materials:

- Quilling paper strips
- Quilling tool (slotted or needle)
- Adhesive

Steps:

1. Start with a quilling paper strip.

2. Coil the strip around the quilling tool, leaving a small tail at one end.

3. Slide the coil off the tool and pinch one side to create a teardrop shape.

4. Repeat the process with another strip, but this time pinch the opposite side to create a mirrored teardrop shape.

5. Attach the two teardrop shapes together at the pinched ends to form an S-scroll.

6. Apply adhesive to secure the S-scroll in place.

Husking Technique

Materials:

- Quilling paper strips
- Quilling tool (slotted or needle)
- Adhesive
- Husking board (optional)

Steps:

1. Start with a quilling paper strip and fold it in half lengthwise.

2. Use the quilling tool to coil one end of the folded strip, leaving the other end uncoiled.

3. Repeat the process with additional strips, coiling them around the first coil in a concentric pattern.

4. Adjust the coils as needed to create symmetrical shapes.

5. Apply adhesive to the uncoiled ends of the strips to secure the husked design.

6. Optionally, use a husking board to help maintain uniformity and spacing between the coils.

Quilled Monograms or Letters

Materials:

- Quilling paper strips
- Quilling tool (slotted or needle)
- Adhesive
- Template or stencil of desired letter/monogram

Steps:

1. Trace or draw the desired letter or monogram onto a piece of paper.

2. Cut quilling paper strips to appropriate lengths for each section of the letter.

3. Use the traced letter as a guide to shape and coil the paper strips into the corresponding sections.

4. Arrange and adhere the quilled pieces onto the traced letter, following its outline.

5. Fill in any gaps or spaces with additional quilled shapes or coils.
6. Allow the adhesive to dry completely before handling the quilled monogram.

These intermediate techniques will expand your quilling repertoire and allow you to create more intricate and detailed designs. Experiment with different variations and combinations to add depth and complexity to your quilled creations!

CHAPTER 4

Advanced Project

Quilled Filigree

Materials:

- Quilling paper strips
- Quilling tool (slotted or needle)
- Adhesive
- Template or pattern for intricate designs

- Tweezers (optional)

Steps:

1. Choose a complex design or pattern as a template.

2. Cut quilling paper strips into various lengths and widths according to the design.

3. Use the template as a guide to shape and coil the paper strips into intricate motifs, scrolls, and flourishes.

4. Layer and assemble the quilled pieces according to the template, paying attention to detail and symmetry.

5. Use tweezers to manipulate and place smaller quilled elements with precision.

6. Adhere each piece carefully to the base or to other quilled elements using adhesive.

7. Allow the adhesive to dry completely before handling the quilled filigree design.

Quilled Lacework

Materials:

- Quilling paper strips
- Quilling tool (slotted or needle)
- Adhesive
- Template or pattern for lacework designs
- Fine-tip glue applicator or quilling needle

Steps:

1. Select a lacework design or pattern as a template.

2. Cut quilling paper strips into thin, delicate strips for the lacework details.

3. Coil and shape the paper strips according to the template, focusing on creating intricate loops, curves, and swirls.

4. Use a fine-tip glue applicator or quilling needle to apply adhesive to the back of each quilled lace element.

5. Carefully adhere the quilled lace pieces onto a base or background, following the design template.

6. Fill in any gaps or spaces with additional quilled elements as needed.7. Allow the adhesive to dry completely before handling the quilled lacework.

Quilled Mosaics:

Materials:

- Quilling paper strips
- Quilling tool (slotted or needle)
- Adhesive
- Base for mosaic (canvas, wood panel, etc.)
- Template or pattern for mosaic design (optional)

Steps:

1. Choose a base for your quilled mosaic, such as a canvas or wood panel.

2. If desired, create or use a template for the mosaic design.

3. Cut quilling paper strips into small, uniform pieces for the mosaic tiles.

4. Arrange the quilled paper pieces on the base according to the design or pattern, creating a mosaic effect.

5. Apply adhesive to the back of each quilled tile and press it firmly onto the base.

6. Continue adding quilled tiles until the entire design is filled in.

7. Allow the adhesive to dry completely before displaying or framing the quilled mosaic.

Quilled Sculptures

Materials:

- Quilling paper strips
- Quilling tool (slotted or needle)
- Adhesive
- Armature or base for sculpture support (wire, foam, etc.)

Steps:

1. Create a basic structure or armature for your quilled sculpture using wire, foam, or other materials.

2. Cut quilling paper strips into various lengths and widths for the sculptural elements.

3. Coil, shape, and manipulate the paper strips to form intricate details and textures for the sculpture.

4. Attach the quilled elements to the armature using adhesive, layering and overlapping them as needed.

5. Build up the sculpture gradually, adding more quilled elements to achieve the desired shape and dimension.

6. Allow the adhesive to dry completely before handling or displaying the quilled sculpture.

Quilled Quilt Patterns

Materials:

- Quilling paper strips
- Quilling tool (slotted or needle)
- Adhesive
- Base for quilt pattern (cardstock, foam board, etc.)
- Template or pattern for quilt design

Steps:

1. Choose a base for your quilled quilt pattern, such as cardstock or foam board.

2. Select a quilt design or pattern as a template for your quilled creation.

3. Cut quilling paper strips into various lengths and widths for the quilt blocks and borders.

4. Arrange the quilled paper strips on the base according to the quilt design, mimicking fabric patterns and textures.
5. Use adhesive to attach the quilled strips to the base, layering and overlapping them as necessary.

6. Fill in the entire base with quilled elements to complete the quilt pattern.

7. Allow the adhesive to dry completely before handling or displaying the quilled quilt pattern.

These advanced techniques will push the boundaries of your quilling skills and allow you to create stunning, intricate works of art. Experiment with different designs, patterns, and materials to unleash your creativity and imagination!

Tips for Success

1. **Practice Regularly**: Like any skill, paper quilling improves with practice. Dedicate time to quilling regularly to refine your techniques and develop your style.

2. **Start Simple**: Begin with basic shapes and techniques before progressing to more complex designs. Mastering the fundamentals will build a strong foundation for your quilling journey.

3. **Use Quality Materials**: Invest in good-quality quilling paper strips and adhesive to ensure the longevity and durability of your quilled creations.

4. **Experiment with Colors and Combinations**: Explore different color combinations and paper widths to add depth and visual interest to your quilled designs.

5. **Precision is Key**: Pay attention to detail and strive for precision in your quilling work. Consistency in size, shape, and spacing will elevate the overall quality of your creations.

6. **Embrace Mistakes**: Don't be afraid to make mistakes, as they can lead to unexpected discoveries and creative breakthroughs. Learn from them and use them as opportunities for growth.

7. **Explore New Techniques**: Challenge yourself to learn new techniques and expand your quilling repertoire. Experiment with advanced techniques to push the boundaries of your creativity.

8. **Seek Inspiration**: Draw inspiration from various sources such as nature, art, and culture. Explore quilling books, blogs, and social media for ideas and inspiration.

9. **Patience and Perseverance**: Quilling requires patience and perseverance, especially when working on intricate designs. Take your time and enjoy the process of creating.

10. **Share Your Work**: Share your quilled creations with others, whether it's through social media, online galleries, or local craft fairs. Celebrate your achievements and inspire others with your passion for quilling.

By following these tips and staying dedicated to your craft, you'll achieve success and fulfillment in your paper quilling journey. Enjoy the creative journey ahead!

CHAPTER 5

Beginner Project

Quilled Flower Greeting Card:

Materials:

- Quilling paper strips (assorted colors)
- Quilling tool (slotted or needle)
- Adhesive
- Cardstock or blank greeting card

Steps:

1. Choose a color for the flower petals and another color for the flower center.

2. Roll two or three tight coils of the chosen petal color to create flower petals.

3. Shape each coil into a teardrop or oval shape by pinching one end.

4. Arrange the petals in a circular pattern on the cardstock, with the pinched ends meeting in the center.

5. Roll a small tight coil of the center color for the flower's center and adhere it to the middle of the petals.

6. Use green quilling strips to create stems and leaves, adhering them to the cardstock below the flower.

7. Allow the adhesive to dry completely before writing a message inside the card.

Quilled Heart Pendant:

Materials:
- Quilling paper strips (assorted colors)
- Quilling tool (slotted or needle)
- Adhesive
- Jewelry findings (e.g., jump ring, necklace chain)
- Clear sealant (optional)

Steps:

1. Choose two complementary colors for the heart pendant.

2. Roll a tight coil of one color and shape it into a teardrop or heart shape for the outer border of the pendant.

3. Roll a smaller tight coil of the second color for the inner part of the heart.

4. Adhere the smaller coil inside the larger coil to complete the heart shape.

5. Use a small strip of quilling paper to create a loop at the top of the heart for attaching the jump ring.

6. Apply adhesive to the back of the heart pendant and attach it to a jump ring.

7. Allow the pendant to dry completely before attaching it to a necklace chain.

8. Optionally, apply a clear sealant to the pendant for added durability.

Quilled Butterfly Magnet:

Materials:

- Quilling paper strips (assorted colors)
- Quilling tool (slotted or needle)
- Adhesive
- Magnet sheet or adhesive magnet backing

Steps:

1. Choose two colors for the butterfly's wings and body.

2. Roll two tight coils of one color for the butterfly's wings.

3. Shape each coil into a teardrop or oval shape for the wings.

4. Roll a small tight coil of the second color for the butterfly's body.

5. Adhere the body coil between the wings coils to complete the butterfly shape.

6. Use small strips of quilling paper to create antennae for the butterfly.

7. Apply adhesive to the back of the butterfly and attach it to the magnet sheet or adhesive magnet backing.

8. Allow the adhesive to dry completely before displaying the butterfly magnet on a fridge or magnetic surface.

Quilled Spiral Earrings:

Materials:

- Quilling paper strips (assorted colors)
- Quilling tool (slotted or needle)
- Adhesive
- Earring hooks
- Jump rings (optional)
- Clear sealant (optional)

Steps:

1. Choose a color for the earrings and roll two tight coils of quilling paper.

2. Gently press down on each coil to flatten it slightly and create a spiral shape.

3. Apply adhesive to the back of each spiral and attach it to an earring hook.

4. Optionally, use jump rings to attach the spirals to the earring hooks for added movement.

5. Allow the adhesive to dry completely before wearing the quilled spiral earrings.

6. Optionally, apply a clear sealant to the earrings for added durability.

Quilled Bookmark:

Materials:

Quilling paper strips (assorted colors)
Quilling tool (slotted or needle)
Adhesive
Cardstock or heavy paper

Steps:

1. Choose a color for the bookmark base and cut a strip of cardstock or heavy paper to your desired size.

2. Choose two or three additional colors for the quilled design.

3. Roll tight coils of quilling paper in various sizes and colors to create decorative shapes.

4. Arrange the quilled shapes on the bookmark base in a pattern or design of your choice.

5. Adhere the quilled shapes to the bookmark base using adhesive.

6. Optionally, add a tassel or ribbon to the top of the bookmark for decoration.

7. Allow the adhesive to dry completely before using the quilled bookmark in your favorite book.

These beginner projects will help you practice basic quilling techniques while creating beautiful and functional crafts. Experiment with colors, shapes, and designs to customize each project to your liking!

CHAPTER 6

Intermediate Project

Quilled Paper Wall Art:

Materials:
- Quilling paper strips (assorted colors)
- Quilling tool (slotted or needle)
- Adhesive
- Canvas or heavy paper
- Frame (optional)

Steps:

1. Choose a design for your wall art, such as a floral motif or abstract pattern.
2. Cut quilling paper strips into various lengths and widths to create the elements of your design.

3. Use quilling techniques like rolling, coiling, and shaping to create the desired shapes and forms.

4. Arrange the quilled elements on the canvas or heavy paper, following your chosen design.

5. Adhere the quilled elements to the surface using adhesive, ensuring they are securely attached.

6. Optionally, frame the quilled wall art for display.

Quilled Paper Jewelry Box:

Materials:

- Quilling paper strips (assorted colors)
- Quilling tool (slotted or needle)
- Adhesive
- Small wooden or cardboard box
- Fabric lining (optional)

Steps:

1. Choose a small box to decorate with quilled paper.
2. Cut quilling paper strips into various lengths and widths for the decorative elements.

3. Use quilling techniques to create coils, spirals, and other shapes for the design.

4. Arrange the quilled elements on the lid and sides of the box in a pleasing pattern.

5. Adhere the quilled elements to the box using adhesive, ensuring they are securely attached.

6. Optionally, line the interior of the box with fabric for a finished look.

Quilled Paper Coasters:

Materials:

- Quilling paper strips (assorted colors)
- Quilling tool (slotted or needle)
- Adhesive
- Cork coasters or heavy cardstock
- Clear sealant

Steps:

1. Choose cork coasters or heavy cardstock as the base for your coasters.

2. Cut quilling paper strips into various lengths and widths for the coaster design.

3. Use quilling techniques to create coils, spirals, and other shapes for the coaster embellishments.

4. Arrange the quilled elements on the coasters in a pattern or design of your choice.

5. Adhere the quilled elements to the coasters using adhesive, ensuring they are securely attached.

6. Apply a clear sealant to the coasters to protect the quilled design from moisture and wear.

Quilled Paper Photo Frame:

Materials:

- Quilling paper strips (assorted colors)
- Quilling tool (slotted or needle)
- Adhesive
- Wooden or cardboard photo frame
- Clear sealant

Steps:
1. Choose a wooden or cardboard photo frame to decorate with quilled paper.

2. Cut quilling paper strips into various lengths and widths for the frame embellishments.

3. Use quilling techniques to create coils, scrolls, and other shapes for the frame design.

4. Arrange the quilled elements on the frame in a pattern or design of your choice.
5. Adhere the quilled elements to the frame using adhesive, ensuring they are securely attached.

6. Apply a clear sealant to the frame to protect the quilled design from moisture and wear.

Quilled Paper Gift Tags:

Materials:

- Quilling paper strips (assorted colors)
- Quilling tool (slotted or needle)
- Adhesive
- Cardstock or heavy paper
- Ribbon or twine

Steps:

1. Choose cardstock or heavy paper to create gift tags.

2. Cut quilling paper strips into various lengths and widths for the tag decorations.

3. Use quilling techniques to create coils, loops, and other shapes for the tag embellishments.
4. Arrange the quilled elements on the tags in a pattern or design of your choice.

5. Adhere the quilled elements to the tags using adhesive, ensuring they are securely attached.

6. Punch a hole at the top of each tag and thread ribbon or twine through for hanging.

These intermediate projects will help you further develop your quilling skills while creating beautiful and functional crafts. Experiment with colors, shapes, and designs to customize each project to your liking!

CHAPTER 7

Advanced project

Quilled Mandala Wall Art:

Materials:

- Quilling paper strips (assorted colors)
- Quilling tool (slotted or needle)
- Adhesive

- Canvas or heavy paper
- Frame (optional)

Steps:

1. Choose a circular canvas or heavy paper as the base for your mandala.

2. Cut quilling paper strips into various lengths and widths for the mandala design.

3. Use intricate quilling techniques like filigree, husking, and fringing to create detailed patterns and motifs.

4. Arrange the quilled elements on the canvas in a symmetrical mandala design.
5. Adhere the quilled elements to the canvas using adhesive, ensuring they are securely attached.

6. Optionally, frame the quilled mandala for display.

Quilled 3D Sculpture:

Materials:

- Quilling paper strips (assorted colors)
- Quilling tool (slotted or needle)
- Adhesive
- Armature or base for sculpture support (wire, foam, etc.)

Steps:

1. Create a wire or foam armature as the foundation for your 3D sculpture.

2. Cut quilling paper strips into various lengths and widths for the sculptural elements.

3. Use advanced quilling techniques to create intricate details and textures for the sculpture.

4. Attach the quilled elements to the armature using adhesive, building up the sculpture gradually.

5. Experiment with layering, shaping, and dimensionality to achieve the desired effect.

6. Allow the adhesive to dry completely before handling or displaying the quilled sculpture.

Quilled Paper Filigree Jewelry Set:

Materials:

- Quilling paper strips (assorted colors)
- Quilling tool (slotted or needle)
- Adhesive
- Jewelry findings (e.g., earring hooks, necklace chain)
- Clear sealant (optional)

Steps:

1. Choose a design for your jewelry set, such as earrings and a necklace pendant.

2. Cut quilling paper strips into various lengths and widths for the jewelry components.

3. Use intricate quilling techniques like filigree and coiling to create detailed patterns and shapes.

4. Arrange the quilled elements to form the desired jewelry pieces, such as floral motifs or geometric designs.
5. Adhere the quilled elements to earring hooks and necklace chains using adhesive.

6. Optionally, apply a clear sealant to the quilled jewelry for added durability and protection.

Quilled Paper Quilt Wall Hanging:

Materials:

- Quilling paper strips (assorted colors)
- Quilling tool (slotted or needle)
- Adhesive
- Fabric backing
- Hanging rod or dowel

Steps:

1. Choose a design for your paper quilt, such as a traditional quilt block pattern.

2. Cut quilling paper strips into various lengths and widths for the quilt blocks and borders.

3. Use advanced quilling techniques to create intricate patterns and designs for each quilt block.

4. Arrange the quilled elements on a fabric backing, following the chosen quilt pattern.

5. Adhere the quilled elements to the fabric backing using adhesive, ensuring they are securely attached.

6. Attach a hanging rod or dowel to the top of the fabric backing for display.

Quilled Paper Clock:

Materials:

- Quilling paper strips (assorted colors)
- Quilling tool (slotted or needle)
- Adhesive
- Clock mechanism
- Wooden or cardboard clock base

Steps:

1. Choose a wooden or cardboard base for your quilled clock.

2. Cut quilling paper strips into various lengths and widths for the clock face and numbers.

3. Use advanced quilling techniques to create intricate designs and patterns for the clock face.

4. Arrange the quilled elements on the clock base, including numbers and decorative elements.

5. Adhere the quilled elements to the clock base using adhesive, ensuring they are securely attached.

6. Attach the clock mechanism to the center of the clock base, following the manufacturer's instructions.

These advanced projects will challenge your quilling skills and creativity while allowing you to create stunning and unique works of art. Experiment with different techniques, designs, and materials to customize each project to your liking!

Troubleshooting and solutions

1. **Loose Coils or Unraveling**:

Issue: The coils in your quilled designs are coming undone or unraveling.

Solution:

- Ensure that you're applying enough adhesive to the end of each paper strip before rolling to secure the coil. Additionally, allow the adhesive to dry completely before handling the quilled piece.

- Consider using a stronger adhesive or applying a small amount of clear glue over the finished coil for extra reinforcement.

2. **Inconsistent Coil Sizes**:

Issue: Your quilled coils vary in size, resulting in an uneven or messy appearance.

Solution:

- Practice rolling the paper strips evenly and consistently using gentle pressure. Use a quilling board with grid lines to help achieve uniform coil sizes.

- Pay attention to the tension applied while rolling to maintain consistency. Trim any excess length from the paper strip before rolling to ensure all coils start at the same size.

3. **Adhesive Residue or Smudges:**

Issue: Excess adhesive leaves behind residue or smudges on your quilled designs.

Solution:

- Use a fine-tip glue applicator or toothpick to apply a thin, even layer of adhesive to the paper strips.

- Avoid applying too much adhesive, as it can seep out and create smudges. Allow the adhesive to dry completely before handling the quilled piece to prevent smudging. Wipe away any excess adhesive with a clean, dry cloth or cotton swab.

4. **Paper Strips Curling or Warping:**

Issue: The paper strips used for quilling are curling or warping, making it difficult to work with them.

Solution:
- Store your quilling paper strips in a cool, dry place away from moisture and direct sunlight to prevent curling or warping.

- Use a heavy object or quilling tool to flatten any curled strips before quilling. If the paper strips become too warped, lightly mist them with water and then press them between heavy books to flatten them out.

5. **Difficulty Shaping Complex Designs:**

Issue: You're struggling to shape intricate or complex designs with your quilled pieces.

Solution:

- Break down complex designs into smaller, more manageable components and assemble them gradually. Use a quilling mold, shaping tools, or your fingers to help shape and manipulate the paper strips into the desired forms. Practice patience and take your time when shaping intricate details, adjusting as needed to achieve the desired outcome.

By addressing these common troubleshooting scenarios and implementing the suggested solutions, you can overcome challenges in your paper quilling projects and create beautiful, high-quality quilled designs. Remember that practice, patience, and attention to detail are key to mastering the art of paper quilling.

Conclusion

In conclusion, paper quilling is a versatile and rewarding art form that offers endless possibilities for creativity. From simple coils to intricate designs, quilling allows artists to express themselves in unique and beautiful ways. Throughout this guide, we've explored various techniques, projects, and troubleshooting tips to help you embark on your quilling journey with confidence.

Starting with basic projects, beginners can learn the fundamentals of quilling and gradually progress to more advanced techniques and designs. With practice, patience, and experimentation, quillers can create stunning works of art, from intricate mandalas to three-dimensional sculptures.

Quilling not only provides a creative outlet but also offers therapeutic benefits, promoting relaxation, focus, and mindfulness. Whether you're crafting greeting cards, jewelry, or home décor, each quilled creation is a testament to your imagination and skill. Happy quilling!